_012

Exploring
Space

NASA

by Martha E. H. Rustad

Consulting Editor: Gail Saunders-Smith, PhD

Consultant: Ilia Iankov Roussev, PhD
Associate Astronomer & Associate Professor
Institute for Astronomy, University of Hawaii at Manoa

CAPSTONE PRESS
a capstone imprint

Pebble Plus is published by Capstone Press,
1710 Roe Crest Drive, North Mankato, Minnesota 56003.
www.capstonepub.com

Books published by Capstone Press are manufactured with paper
containing at least 10 percent post-consumer waste.

Library of Congress Cataloging-in-Publication Data
Rustad, Martha E. H. (Martha Elizabeth Hillman), 1975–
 NASA / by Martha E. H. Rustad.
   p. cm.—(Pebble plus. Exploring space)
 Includes bibliographical references and index.
 Summary: "Full-color photographs and simple text describe the National Aeronautics and Space Administration"—
Provided by publisher.
 ISBN 978-1-4296-7581-9 (library binding)
 ISBN 978-1-4296-7894-0 (paperback)
 1. United States. National Aeronautics and Space Administration—Juvenile literature. 2. Astronautics—United
States—Juvenile literature. 3. Outer space—Exploration—United States—Juvenile literature. I. Title.
 TL521.312.R87 2012
 629.40973—dc23   2011021645

Editorial Credits
Erika L. Shores, editor; Alison Thiele, designer; Kathy McColley, production specialist

Photo Credits
NASA, cover, 5, 7, 11, 13, 17, 21, JPL, 15, Kim Shiflett, 9, Regan Geeseman, 19
NASA/U.S. Army White Sands Missile Range, 1

Artistic Effects
Shutterstock: glossygirl21, Primož Cigler, SmallAtomWorks

Note to Parents and Teachers

The Exploring Space series supports national science standards related to earth science. This
book describes and illustrates NASA. The images support early readers in understanding the
text. The repetition of words and phrases helps early readers learn new words. This book
also introduces early readers to subject-specific vocabulary words, which are defined in the
Glossary section. Early readers may need assistance to read some words and to use the Table of
Contents, Glossary, Read More, Internet Sites, and Index sections of the book.

Printed in the United States of America in North Mankato, Minnesota.

102011   006405CGS12

Table of Contents

What Is NASA?

Have you ever built a robot?

Would you like to launch

a rocket into space?

People who work for NASA

do these jobs every day.

NASA stands for National Aeronautics and Space Administration.

NASA is part of the U.S. government.

NASA's main office is in

Washington, D.C. Other offices

are throughout the country,

and even in space.

Mission Control Center,
Johnson Space Center, Houston, Texas

At NASA people study space
and how to get there.
In Ohio workers design
new spacecraft. In Florida
NASA workers launch spacecraft.

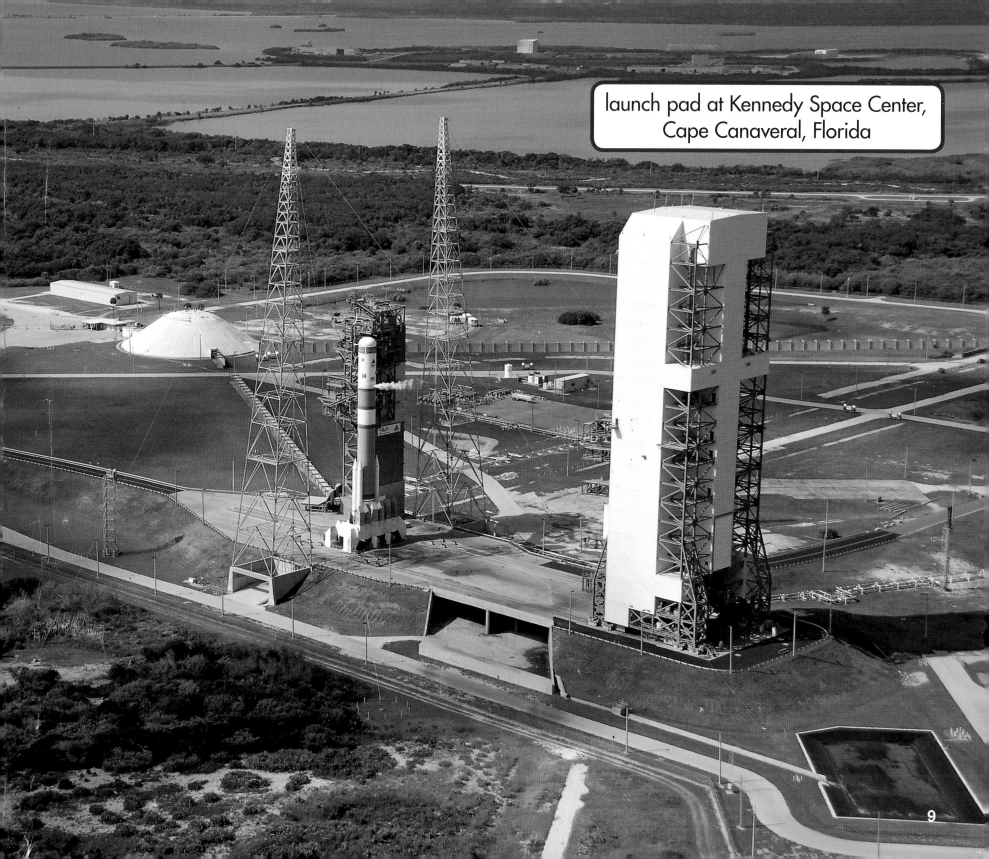

launch pad at Kennedy Space Center,
Cape Canaveral, Florida

Astronauts train for space travel.
Some NASA workers make sure
astronauts have air to breathe.
Others make sure they have
water to drink and food to eat.

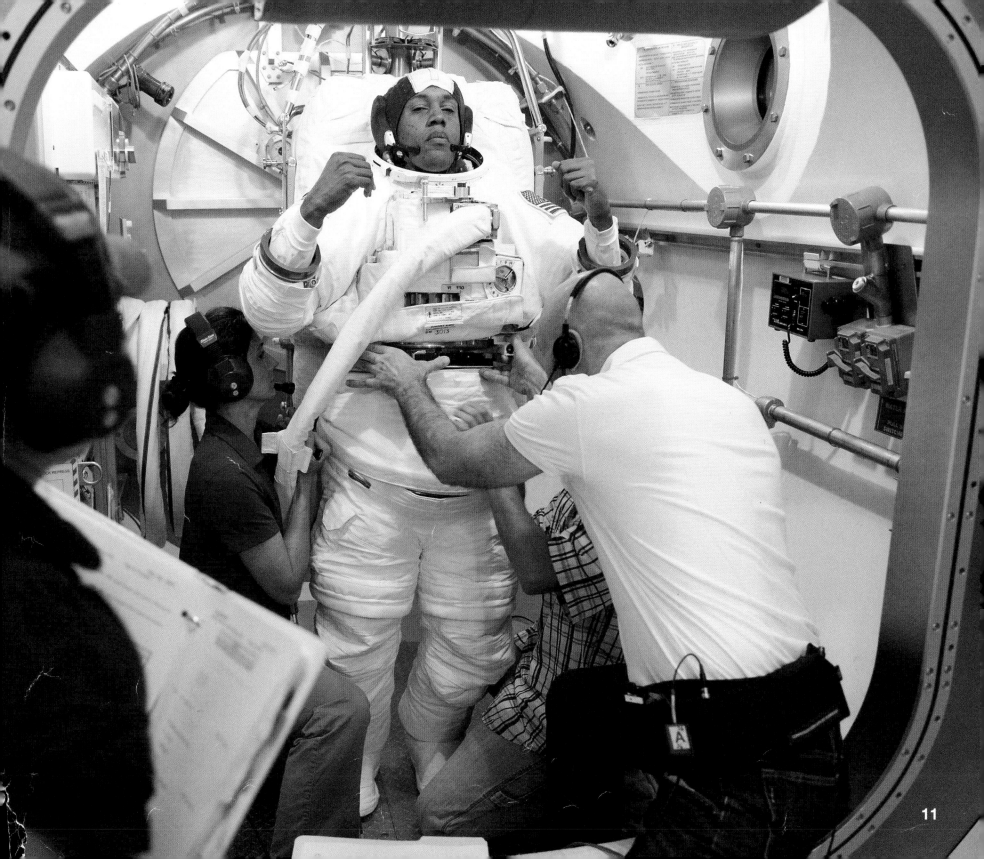

Spacecraft and Robots

NASA uses all kinds of tools to study space. Probes explore other planets. Satellites orbit Earth. A space station lets astronauts live and work in outer space.

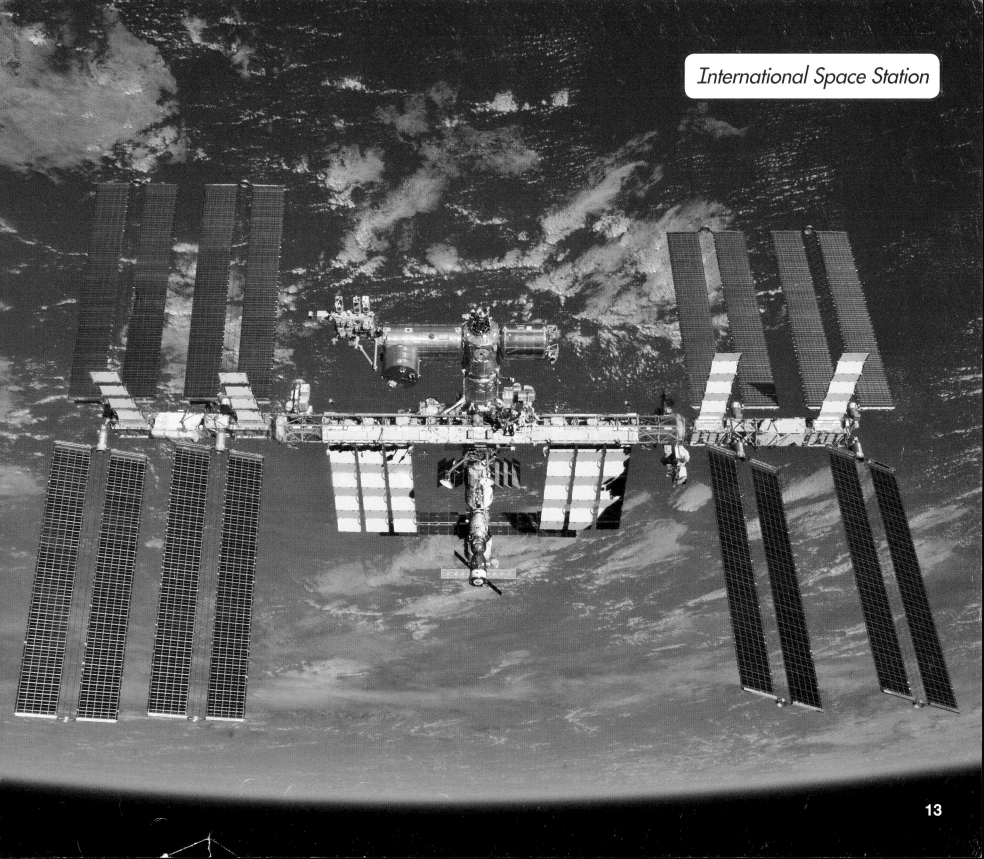

International Space Station

Space is dangerous. There's no safe air to breathe and everything floats. NASA uses rovers and robots to do some jobs more safely than humans.

NASA built a robot called Robonaut 2, or R2. R2 works inside the *International Space Station*. Someday R2 may help astronauts work on the moon and even Mars.

The Future of NASA

Workers at NASA are building
new spacecraft and rovers.
NASA plans to explore the moon
and even send astronauts
to an asteroid or Mars.

future moon rover

NASA will keep studying space.

Satellites with telescopes

continue to take pictures

of faraway stars. Maybe NASA

will even find life on other planets.

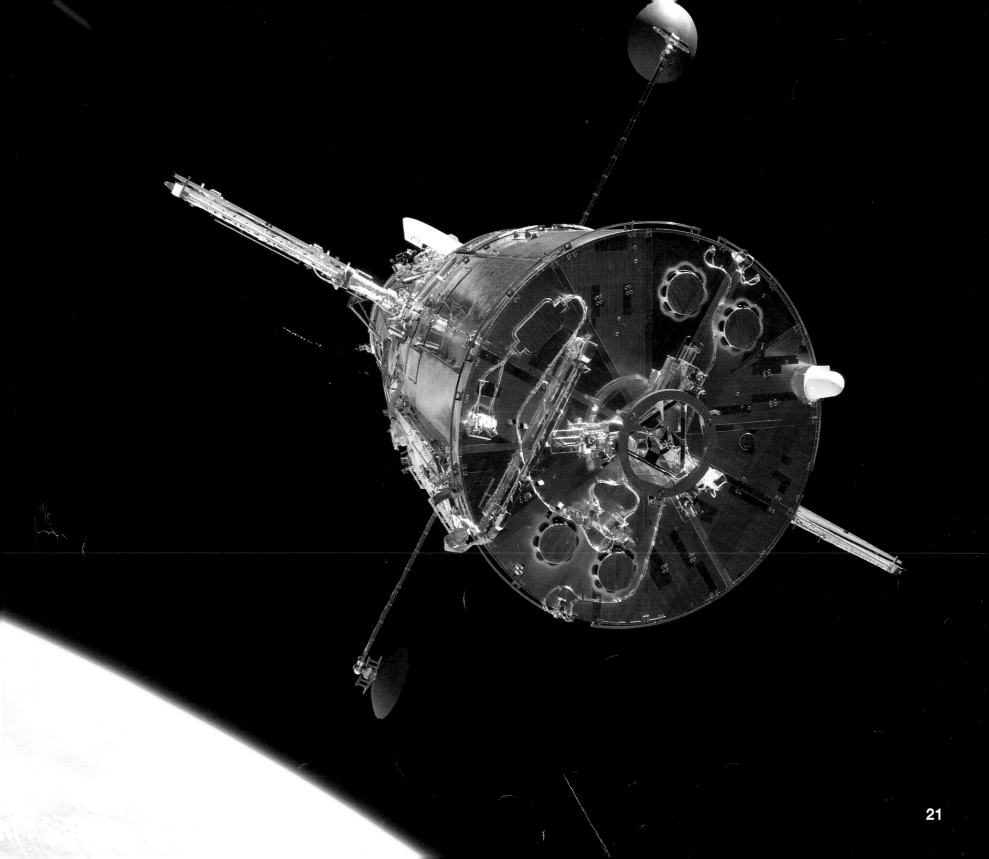

Glossary

orbit—to travel around an object in space

probe—a small vehicle used to explore objects in outer space

rocket—a long, tube-shaped object that moves by pushing fuel from one end

rover—a small vehicle that people can move by using remote control

satellite—a spacecraft that circles Earth

space station—a spacecraft that circles Earth in which astronauts can live for long periods of time

telescope—a tool people use to look at planets and other objects in space; telescopes make planets and other objects look closer than they really are

Read More

Rustad, Martha E. H. *Space Stations.* Exploring Space. Mankato, Minn.: Capstone Press, 2012.

Zappa, Marcia. *NASA.* The Universe. Edina, Minn.: ABDO, 2011.

Zobel, Derek. *NASA.* Blastoff! Readers: Exploring Space. Minneapolis: Bellwether Media, 2010.

Internet Sites

FactHound offers a safe, fun way to find Internet sites related to this book. All of the sites on FactHound have been researched by our staff.

Here's all you do:

Visit *www.facthound.com*

Type in this code: 9781429675819

Super-cool stuff! Check out projects, games and lots more at **www.capstonekids.com**

Index

Word Count: 226
Grade: 1
Early-Intervention Level: 22